TRACKS:
POEMS ON THE "L"

poems by

Lois Baer Barr

Finishing Line Press
Georgetown, Kentucky

TRACKS: POEMS ON THE "L"

New Women's Voices Series, No. 170

Copyright © 2022 by Lois Baer Barr
ISBN 979-8-88838-053-6 First Edition
All rights reserved under International and Pan-American Copyright Conventions. No part of this book may be reproduced in any manner whatsoever without written permission from the publisher, except in the case of brief quotations embodied in critical articles and reviews.

ACKNOWLEDGMENTS

Thanks to the editors of the publications and media where the following poems have appeared in slightly different versions:

"Rainy Day on the 'L'" in the *Chicago Tribune*, September 16, 2019.
"Reading Maoist Poetry: A Review" online at *Highland Park Poetry* 2019.
"Mass Transit" aired on the news show, "Good Day DePaul," on October 22, 2019, available on Vimeo.
"at home" was published in Spanish at *Letralia*, Papeles de la pandemia.
    24 años de *Letralia*, April 2020 https://letralia.com/editorial/especiales/letralia24/
"Edgewater Studio," "Mass Transit," "Woman May Go Blind," "How We Dance," "Fail Better I and II" and "At Home" were read online in an interview on Youtube with editor Tim Green on *Rattlecast* March 23, 2021 https://www.facebook.com/watchlive/?v=945219276251851&ref=watch_permalink Also available on iTunes, Sound Cloud and Spotify.

Publisher: Leah Huete de Maines
Editor: Christen Kincaid
Cover Art: Lew Barr
Author Photo: Lew Barr
Cover Design: Elizabeth Maines McCleavy

Order online: www.finishinglinepress.com
    also available on amazon.com

Author inquiries and mail orders:
Finishing Line Press
PO Box 1626
Georgetown, Kentucky 40324
USA

Table of Contents

Edgewater Studio 1

mass transit 2

Rainy Day on the "L" 3

Reading Buddies at George Manierre School 4

Social Science Study I 6

Social Science Study II 7

The Patty Crowley Apartments 8

Rapid Transit Circa 1897 9

Cabrini Green I 10

Cabrini Green II 11

Reading Poetry about Maoist China: A Review 12

Dare on the "L" I 13

Dare on the "L" II 14

Woman May Go Blind After Attack 15

Take Me Out to the Ball Game 16

Inauguration Day 17

Off 18

Today I worry 19

How We Dance 20

Fail Better I 21

Gentle Reader, ... 22

at home 25

Fail Better II 26

Sources 27

With Thanks 28

Invocation

Edgewater Studio
January 13, 2019

Bless this early morning place, the whir
of the fridge, the whoosh of elevated trains
one block east, the organic Peruvian coffee,
the long-legged writer who enters quietly.
He outsteps me.
The little bathroom we keep tidy
and the untidy row of books we've written.
Signs everywhere, from the prices
of artwork to kitchen notices:
—*We do not want a mouse to be welcome.*
I nibble on toast, daydream, sip coffee,
plan what I'll write later today.

Zip my parka.
Rush outdoors to catch the "L."

mass transit

they assemble to ride
        bundles on their backs
in their hands
        phones, kindles, a binder
of choral music, the *Chicago Tribune*
a young man's lips move through
        The Alchemist
they share sniffles and coughs
        unscheduled stops between stations
tolerate riders sleeping
        on three seats
who ride the train to survive
        it's twenty below
many offer me a seat I refuse
unless I'm scribbling
        sitting is death

Rainy Day

walk to Bryn Mawr Station
gray suede rain-proofed boots
Chicago Botanic Garden umbrella

I stare down the long gray line
*—we are waiting for a signal
to resume momentarily*

black bag of books
black clouds loom
I board

damp passengers
drippy umbrellas
musty smells

*—check to see you have
all your belongings
before you exit*

—Sedgwick is next
a two-block walk
to Manierre School

reading buddies
give dap   laughter
expels the gloom

Reading Buddies at George Manierre School

The old buddies don't ask
young buddies questions,
but they tell us things. Brandy's
excited to have Thanksgiving
turkey for the first time.
Comes back sad,
—*We had to pitch it.*
It smelled so bad.
We don't ask whether dads are at home.
We ignore the blue shirts getting
grimy after two weeks.

Brandy has long eye lashes,
a rhinestone stud in one ear,
dreadlocks and a huge smile.
First day Brandy read
Today I Will Fly.
Stumbled on the elephant's name,
Gerald, but got Piggie right.
—*Yes ma'am!* I said.
—*Hey, I'm a boy!* he cried.

Brandy earns a free book,
picks *Barbie* for his sister.
I wonder if he's too soft,
but he wins at arm wrestling.

Lamart is smart and he knows it.
He tackles *Who Is Barack Obama?*
Enjoys words like *Afghanistan*
and *Punahou* (Barack's school).
He draws a self-portrait
cross hatches the shading.
Beats me at Hang Man
and Bananagrams.
Sneaks into the room
to make me think he didn't come,
but he always does.

Second grade bores him.
In June he's mad about stuff
at home or at me
because the year is ending.

Next year I'll have new buddies.
—*Will you come see me?* I ask both.
Brandy says yes, but Lamart says no.
—*What if I bring you books?*
He grins. Gives me hope.

Social Science Study I

I'm keeping track of riders who use electronic devices versus readers of paper on the Red Line of the "L" at the Bryn Mawr Station at 8:40 a.m. Though people offer me their seats prompted, no doubt, by the announcement—*Priority seating is for the elderly and disabled*—for the sake of the study, I stand.

Don't trust my numbers. I get distracted. Today I decided 8/8 was the meter of the wheels along the track and anyway sometimes the car is crowded, and at my height I can only study the shoes. I was dying to ask this guy with tweedy wool sneakers where he got them or ask the slender guy in fatigues where he's been deployed. He was studying instructions to Union Station.

Social Science Study II

I watch for the greening of trees at parks and Graceland Cemetery, but I need to focus on the readers of books versus readers on cell phones and kindles. I realize I can't go up to each one to see whether they're playing Candy Crunch or reading *War and Peace*. Anyway, something will surely distract me, and since I'm keeping the numbers in my head, I can only give an estimated interim report. On fourteen rides in April and May of 2019, 19% of riders read on paper, 78% use electronic devices, and 3% just doze, stare into space or people watch. Next year I can track purses versus backpacks or how many people, like me, brazenly stare at others.

The Patty Crowley Apartments

adjoin the "L" at Sedgwick
rock to the clatter of the tracks
thirty-nine units for homeless women

Patrick and Patty Crowley raised
five kids and fifty foster children

women from the shelter sit and smoke
on a low wall at the CTA entryway
used mattresses land by the dumpster
in the driveway from time to time

two doors down Sotheby's offers condos
granite kitchens, Juliet balconies, hardwood floors

Rapid Transit Circa 1897

Blackmail sprang him
from prison in Philly.
He bribed Chicago's
city fathers,
bought up land rights,
toppled a governor.
Charles Tyson Yerkes
raised tracks
around the Loop.
Robbing Peter
to pay Paul
he lined his pockets
with millions,
his walls with art.
Yerkes ditched
Midwest bankers,
crossed the pond,
and electrified
London's Tube.

Cabrini Green I

Called "Swede Town" or "Little Hell" in 1860.
Shanties popped up in river lowlands.
Public housing in 1942 kept quotas:
one fourth black to three fourths white.
They named it for Saint Frances Cabrini.
Late fifties, high rises and townhomes rose.
Seventy acres that fifteen thousand called
home. The towers roiled with sniper fire
when Dr. King was killed.
Snipers persisted in the seventies;
drugs, roaches, and rats ravaged residents.

—*Fix it up! Don't tear it down!*
Marion Stamps, once a Black Panther,
organized tenants. —*We stopped
the gang war, then here come Jane Byrne.*
Mayor Byrne moved in, made headlines.
Stamps spied her sneaking out at night.

Wrecking balls flattened towers, shattered
community. The city gave residents an offer
they couldn't refuse. Annie Ricks said
—*I had to go or be homeless again.*

Cabrini Green II

Tom, another reading buddy,
checks his CTA app,
—*We've missed Purple and Brown;
let's get the Red Line at Clybourn.
There's a shortcut.*
We zigzag west of Manierre School.
Potholes, puddles, abandoned
campus, empty soccer fields where
thousands lived stacked in towers.

Flashback: fear of driving here.

Clybourn and North.
Shiny Apple Store.
Fountains, chairs, trees.
Descend steep stairs.
Darkened platform.

Flashback: the rat
that brushed our feet
in a New York subway
then burned on the track.
Chit-chat distracts.

Train ascends to sunlight
at Fullerton. I jump up.
—*No need to transfer.* Tom laughs.

Reading Poetry about Maoist China: A Review

The "L" cannot distract you from Zheng's toil
in leech-filled rice fields hungry as only a boy
just out of high school can be
so hungry the setting sun is a *big tomato*
toothed in half by hills
      a hammered dulcimer daring to play *de-revolutionary songs*
      drowns out a jeremiad against religion from a rider nearby
      despite the roaring motor and the clack of old tracks
you watch the sun become a red dot
then the red eyes of a tired farmer
the glow of his cigarette on a darkened porch.
you sense Zheng's numbness when a peasant announces Mao has died.

Laugh when the poet's ten-year-old tweets from Tiananmen Square,
—*Papa, who's Chairman Mao?*
                    You transfer at Fullerton
          then miss the "S" curve's
                teakettle whistle
             miss the call *Sedgwick is next!*

Dare on the "L" I

Ross Gay dared himself to find delight every day for a year.
    His words spread joy.
I will dare to go beyond my limits every day for a year.
    Can I do it?

Who cares that I'm wearing black silk boxers over my panties
    this snowy Chicago day?
Or that it took me fifty minutes to drive to Edgewater
    park behind the studio
or that the short-order cook at Nookies undercooked
    my fried eggs
or that I dared myself to speak to someone on the "L"

    —*What's your bag mean?*
Her canvas bag trimmed in leather read, HELL YEAH!
    —*I don't know. I like the designer.*
I said it was a great bag and she said thanks.
    End of conversation.
She smiled; her teeth were even and white
    we connected.

Who cares that there were delays on the "L" going north:
    —*Sick passenger.*
Our train heading south was fine; I kept reading Ross Gay's
    Book of Delights
arrived at Manierre School in time to jot this down.

    Does anyone care?
Dammit, I'm the writer, and I'll put train delays,
    Ross Gay,
runny eggs, and silk knickers in my poems
    if I please.

Dare on the "L" II

On the Northbound train, a young man smiles. He speaks before I dare to talk, —*It's really cold today.* I answer, —*Yes. You from Chicago?* Elder Dillman is a missionary from a farm south of Salt Lake City.

—*Are you proud or angry Romney voted to impeach Trump?* I inquire.
—*I'm a member of the Church of the Latter-Day Saints, so I don't watch TV or pay attention to politics.* I apologize. We chat about parkas and boots; I pepper him with questions.

He removes a glove, and I do likewise. We shake hands. I keep up the questions. Is it hard to approach strangers? Are you homesick? A pause. He begins to explain the God who gives us everlasting life if we so choose. I reply,
—*Well, I don't believe in that kind of God, but I do believe we are here for a purpose.* He loves that word purpose, and he talks about finding happiness in God. I say I also don't know about happiness or the choices many people have. I tell him stories of my reading buddies at Manierre School. One lost his favorite uncle to a gun fight, and the other acts out violent super-hero fantasies each time we read. The second boy, I fear, is being hurt by someone close.

Elder Dillman, a boy himself, reaches inside his parka to bring out *The Book.* —*Don't waste a copy. I've read it.* I shake my head. —*When?* I fib, —*In graduate school, a long time ago.* Then add, —*I am Jewish, I read the Old Testament and I've read The New Testament.* He perks up, but I shoot back more questions. At Wilson, he rises to escape, —*This is my stop.* I extend my hand. —*Good luck and God bless you.* He wishes me the same. Any another day I wouldn't dare to ask questions. He would have preached to me. Dillman is off to snare souls at Truman College.

Woman May Go Blind After Attack

at Standard Club's valet stand
I hear this story the first time
a friend of a friend rolls her eyes

when I say I'm catching the "L"
her friend's friend, she says, was punched
in the eye by a rider on the Red Line

women push worldly goods in grocery carts
panhandlers hover   my friend Tom reports
Jarvis Station is a makeshift lavatory

today Tom departs early to buy blueberries,
a tall guy in a hoody scrambles to his seat,
reaches over my head, grabs a postcard,

but when I turn to get one myself,
I discover there is no sign with cards
for the taking   I plan my exit

yesterday 4 p.m. two men
were shot on the Argyle platform
fourteen-year-old boy arrested

I manage the "L" though friends
repeat the tale of the one-eyed woman
I add money to my Ventra card

Take Me Out to the Ball Game

Workshop buddies whine, —*You didn't write about Wrigley Field? Addison is the best stop on the Red Line.* They love to squeeze inside the "L" with other fans in Cubs' wear. Oh dear. I must confess I went to bed when game seven of the 2016 World Series went to overtime. (I know: extra innings.) I despise the domestic violence of players, the corporate nature of baseball, changes in the ballpark's neighborhood. Seats with obstructed view are $42. They don't list the price of suites; if you have to ask, you can't afford them. But, hey, if your friends inherited a box, why not go? When they invite you, park in Wrigleyville if you have money to burn and don't mind massive traffic. Take the "L," unless you're claustrophobic. If you plan to treat your hosts to refreshments, bring a hundred bucks for hot dogs, cracker jack and beer. Or hit the bars afterwards and stay at Hotel Zachary for only $500. Go Cubbies!

Inauguration Day
July 2, 2019

I grab for a pole and the pale girl flinches,
sees me see her cuddle with a raven-haired
girl. I give them space, turn around and stare
at the gap between our car and the platform
as the train departs Argyle Station.
Standing passengers, do not lean against the doors.

I scan other faces. The guy with robin's egg
blue bangs and a big stud in his nose intrigues me.
But the couple are laughing now, so I twist
for a closer look. One's shaved a side of her head,
the other is dressed in black. One wears bedraggled
sandals and the other sneakers. At Belmont
they depart. In seconds I decide not to follow
their lead. Doors close. They lean into a pillar.
Laughing they touch one another's faces,
kiss slowly. *Darn*, I think, *I'll miss the rest.*

That night I nestle with my husband
to watch the news. Mayor Lori Lightfoot
hugs her tall wife after her oath of office.
I recall the lovers and wonder whether
today was their inauguration day too?

Off

At Howard Station a mural of giant fruit
on the back of the old Howard Theatre.
Orange spheres, blue leaves shaped like tongues.
Onions fried in old oil fill the August air.

Northbound train at last. I cross the platform blocked
by a pale man clad in black, black rollaboard suitcase,
gray braid down his back. Greasy tendrils frame
deep circles round his eyes. He sits two seats
down. I turn my head to avoid the smell.

The motorman announces,
Put out that cigarette. I see you.
Put it out, or you'll be off at the next stop.

This sets my neighbor off: *Put it out, man,*
or you'll be shackled and whipped. Get off
now or your identity will be impounded.
He rants to the unknown smoker in another car.
Agent Orange, Viet Cong, conspiracies, piracy,
moon walks, Nixon tapes, vaping, and rape.
Strange ciphers swell to trillions, words spew,
odor grows, but I'm rooted to this spot
'til the train hits Davis. We both get off.

Today I worry

about germs on the handrails, active shooters,
dentist appointments, melting polar icecap, fleas.
I examine the blue tufted seatbacks with care.
A young man with long eyelashes, legs stretched
across the aisle, scratches his thigh vigorously,
so I skip the seat by him
sit by the girl with the long blonde braid
that swishes my shoulder when she turns to chat
in a Slavic tongue to her itchy boyfriend
who jumps up to check the route map, winks
at the chubby kid across from us whose eye is
swollen shut. I wonder what happened and if
the girl by me is the kid's sister? Their hair
is the same color, but I cannot see
her face because she leans into the boyfriend,
who repeats announcements. *Addison is next.
Addison*, he says with a Slavic *Ah*.
Then *Addison* with the flat Chicago "A."
I laugh and forget the fleas.
This young man will speak English in a flash.
But what's to become of the moon-faced boy
and who closed his eye?

How We Dance
March 3, 2020

We kissed minutes after the alarm clock
pulled you from a party with Uncle Lou.
Then we stubbed toes racing to pee.
What an inelegant epithalamium.
Yes, I am sure that's a word.

Sometimes when we kiss, there's static
electricity or we bump noses;
sometimes our bodies know how to connect.
Not when we dance. We both improvise.
We both like to lead, but I followed you
to New York City on a bike.

So here we are decades later
with stubbed toes and tender bruises,
but the kids are great, aren't they?
We pushed through the perils of parenting,
divorces, death of close friends.

Oh, the wines we tasted
walking in Rioja, Tuscany, and Corfu
and the rides along lakes and rivers.
Endurance hikes ending in sunstroke,
on the precipice of cliffs.

Robert Hass revved me up on the "L" today
asking Brenda Hillman if she noticed
"To Be Accompanied by Flute and Zither"
was an anniversary poem?
I didn't until he said that.
I don't think poets should marry,
but Dorianne Laux and others have managed.

So, you line things up, and I like 'em slant;
yet we wouldn't do this dance,
we couldn't do this dance with anyone else.

Fail Better I
March 5, 2020

Kim Addonizio quotes Samuel Beckett
on the 8:50 Brown Line run to the Loop.
Rejections come on weekends,
when editors shed their day jobs.
They sting less as I read
Kim's interview in *Rattle*
to the whine and clatter of wheels.
A fatherly voice reminds me
not to lean against the doors.

I like curves on the "L"
better than curves in life.
Before poetry, Kim studied flute.
A poetic turn.

Try again. Fail again. Fail better.
Seventy-three, I rush up steep stairs
littered with pigeon muck, feathers,
ten below wind chill on platforms,
rides as unpredictable as weather.

And what if I fail anyway?
Few expectations for money, prizes.
Just need to ride out my poems,
tap my Ventra card at the turnstile
'till the green light says, *Go*.

Gentle Reader,

Take me into your hands
and chortle.
Take me to bed with you,
take me in your pocket on the "L,"
dog ear the page of your favorite
poem. Copy it down
for a friend.
Leave me in a café
for someone else.

Yes, I'm an old lady,
but maybe we have something
in common.
Maybe you're too angry to be
gentle. *This woman lives
in a bubble. She has nothing
to say to me.*
Maybe you think I just see your skin,
I do notice it.
I am sorry. I do.
But I want to hear your story,
know you,
want to be your reader too.

Epilogue

at home
March 18, 2020

highway's hum muted
dishwasher has run
washer and dryer wait,
doors agape,
as piles congregate
on the laundry floor
quiet pervades
commute to Chicago approaches
memory's vanishing point
gone the steep stairways, crowded platforms, unreachable straps
gone the woman toting her worldly goods in a cart
the man sleeping on three seats
Graceland Cemetery gone, dog park,
coop gardens, DePaul students at Fullerton, swerves,
wheels' whistle through the long curve east,
writing studio, reading buddies
gone

gray branches crosshatch our berm
the star magnolia where we scattered
our dog's ashes will bloom soon,
its white-flowered beauty
will pierce tender wounds
if we lose another friend now

Fail Better II
March 3, 2021

For Amy Davis

Try again. Fail again. Fail better.
The pandemic puts rejection in perspective.
Payment from a poetry journal,
royalties from my chapbook help.
Two weeks away from Facebook
deflates my ego like it was
on the Red Line: nowhere to expand.

I want to ride the "L" again–
share air space, delays, rattles,
and hums. Sway with other riders.
A poetry petri dish, the "L"
is so full of people's stories,
you cannot fail to find one.

Sources:

Quotes in "Cabrini Green I" from picket lines filmed in documentary, *Seventy Acres in Chicago* and from Marion Stamps interview. http://digital.wustl.edu/e/eii/eiiweb/sta5427.0681.154marc_record_interviewee_process.html

Annie Ricks from https://www.nytimes.com/2018/02/06/magazine/the-towers-came-down-and-with-them-the-promise-of-public-housing.html

"Woman May Go Blind in CTA Attack." Title comes from headline on CBS Local News, June 15, 2018. https://chicago.cbslocal.com/2018/06/15/898672-woman-may-go-blind-cta-attack/

"Reading Maoist Poetry: A Review," Thanks to Jianqing Zheng for permission to quote from his poems in *Enforced Rustication in the Maoist Cultural Revolution* (Texas A & M University Press, 2019).

"Dare on the 'El' I and II" inspired by Ross Gay, *The Book of Delights* (Algonquin Books of Chapel Hill, 2019).

"Today I worry" inspired by stories about motormen, "*Secrets of the Trade: CTA Motormen Tell Their Stories*" https://www.nbcchicago.com/news/local/Secrets-of-the-Trade-CTA-Motormen-Tell-Their-Stories-500319361.html

"How We Dance" is inspired by Robert Hass, "To Be Accompanied by Flute and Zither," *Summer Snow* (HarperCollins, 2020).

"Fail Better I and II" are inspired by Tim Green's interview with Kim Addonizio in *Rattle* #67, Spring 2020 in which she expounds on Samuel Beckett's words.

With Thanks

Here is where I inevitably shall fail to thank the many people who read, corrected, and improved these poems. Bluff Coast Writers—Kathy Dohrmann, Karin Gordon, Cynthia Hahn, and I—have written together for at least a dozen years. Amin Ahmad, Vimi Bajaj, Nada Sneige Fuleihan, Rachel Gottlieb, and Natalia Nebel read the entire collection and made many valuable suggestions. Rachel helped me pitch it to the *Chicago Tribune* where transportation writer Mary Wisniewski published a story about the poetry. Deerfield Library Poets, a weekly workshop led by Herb Berman, M.J. Gabrielsen, and Judith Kaufmann, have read and critiqued most of these poems. Carla Arnell, David George, Richard Mallette (1948-2019), and Gizella Meneses have supported me in so many ways over the years. I am also grateful to poets Ellen Birkett Morris, Jennifer Dotson, Jacquelyn Harris, and Andrea Slotke-Witz. I'm so grateful to my loyal fan Dr. Maceo Ellison. I thank my family—Emily Barr Ruth, Erin Ruth, Norah Ruth, and Judith Wertheim for reading my work. Most of all, I must thank my husband Lew Barr for everything.

Lois Baer Barr was a volunteer for Open Books Chicago as a Reading Buddy at a school in Old Town when most of these poems were written. Author of a chapbook of fiction, *Lope de Vega's Daughter,* and of poetry, *Biopoesis,* Barr is a three-time Pushcart Prize nominee and was a finalist for the Rita Dove Poetry Award. An emerita professor of Spanish at Lake Forest College, she has published critical essays, translations, poetry, and fiction in English and Spanish in journals and anthologies here and abroad. She lives in Riverwoods with her husband Lew. They like to hike and bike.

www.ingramcontent.com/pod-product-compliance
Lightning Source LLC
Chambersburg PA
CBHW022127090426
42743CD00008D/1033